BEARINGS

BEARINGS

✻

STEPHANIE ANDERSON

NEW MICHIGAN PRESS
TUCSON, ARIZONA

NEW MICHIGAN PRESS
DEPT OF ENGLISH, P. O. BOX 210067
UNIVERSITY OF ARIZONA
TUCSON, AZ 85721-0067

<http://newmichiganpress.com>

Orders and queries to <nmp@thediagram.com>.

Copyright © 2024 by Stephanie Anderson. All rights reserved.

ISBN 978-1-934832-95-0. FIRST PRINTING.

Design by Ander Monson.

Cover image by Stephanie Anderson.

CONTENTS

With Love and Dread and Rage and Love,   1
With Love and Love and Rage and Love,   4
With Love and Burrowing and Rage and Love,   6
With Love and Guilt and Rage and Love,   10
With Love and Flight and Rage and Love,   13
With Love and Fear and Rage and Love,   18
With Love and Terror and Rage and Love,   20
With Love and Career and Rage and Love,   25
With Love and Chroma and Rage and Love,   28
With Love and Baths and Rage and Love,   32
With Love and Distance and Rage and Love,   35
With Love and Flight and Rage and Love,   38
With Love and Nice and Rage and Love,   42
With Love and Willfulness and Rage and Love,   44
With Love and Lochia and Rage and Love,   47
With Love and Love and Rage and Love,   54
With Love and Horses and Rage and Love,   55
With Love and Paths and Rage and Love,   57
With Love and Remembering and Rage and Love,   60

Appendix: Dates   67
Appendix: Addressees   68
Notes   69
Acknowledgments   70

WITH LOVE AND DREAD AND RAGE AND LOVE,

Or is it anticipation
        cut perversely

Something must happen

Dear ones, say you
        feel it too

Parts of my body are blank

It's not a wish but it's also
        not Cassandra

I think about the word *era*

I'm working on ferocity
        and frankness:

This poem fails

Here an affect there
        an affect

Let's reclaim *sad*

Is it foreboding if
    it's factual

Okay a little wish

I think about the words
    period of my life

It's an endurance act

Her father dies and I keep
    wading

He has to see the cardiologist

I want to commit to the
    poem but I can't

I get cold and cultivate selfishness

She says *each generation is called
    a word in the poem*

I write *patience* in my notebook

I wait for my period and drink
    a Corona

I try to make it a speech act

Have I given myself permission
        to inhabit my body

I think about the alien inside

I think about the phrase
        unwanted advances

Parts of our bodies are blank

I put my fingers on
        your coronaries

Come at me

WITH LOVE AND LOVE AND RAGE AND LOVE,

Wednesday we discover several things.
First that some consider memory
to be a lilting luxury. *But it's science* you say,

pointing to *reading is the most beautiful
posture.* I agree, I can't explain, I throw it up.

We use several because singularity sounds
like woe. *How can Americans not believe in science*

out the window white water. Lyric sounds
like pretty nation but we're going to spit it up.

Why do I leave furrows in the texts dragging
my bad memory beside. We'll show these men
our lyric. It's not modesty *it hurts* you say

*what they forget. Lyric is supposed to
hurt* he said while I choked it up.

All these minutes of questionable consent.
When I spoke he said *how unfair.*

They sang of sweets as the girl starved.
It's not a simile it's a scene it's not an allegory

it's an event. On the map, great gasps
of land are already gone. When we sleep
we are heaving about power.

WITH LOVE AND BURROWING AND RAGE AND LOVE,

you shambles
    spent climber

    I watch you
race clockwise

and start to get
    an urge

to put the poem
    outside time

I don't wanna
    but how to

    arrange you
ten weeks old

eyes big
    at song

and Donald Trump
    on the page

  with an app
the driver says

your president is
  very humorous

  you touch
the mattress

  pill bug
curl now your

head lolls like
an older child's

will mothering
  make me

  minimalist
often it feels

like I expected
  only more or

  less your
test translates

wild type—normal
    you turn into

a flock of
    geese in

    my arms
prescient

    he came to
Beijing and took

away a lot
    of dollars

I keep turning
    to metaphor

    because I'd
like it easeful

    the *kuàidì*
guys are gone

    you yawn
mouth a black

plum once I
    place this

part the poem
will be over

   or a small
black moon

I await another
   addressee

WITH LOVE AND GUILT AND RAGE AND LOVE,

I keep talking about family
planning in public or in polite
company, too much the same.
Let's keep this one singular.
Beijing gets outrageously humid
and personified, trade war
lewks, a kind of connection.

It's July and it's June,
a road like a river.
I almost let myself be lasered
without anesthesia; it would
be better for the baby.
Little void, crater
where a small sun crashed.

I fret less about ferocity
with you in the house.
Each morning I read headlines,
then bike into another
world, though the students
still argue about whether
poems should convey feelings

or create them. I punch
the air: parataxis. *You could
even call it period style*, I say,
if you were an asshole.
Rain on the roof like
itself somewhere over there.
It's June and then July.

I bike one hand holding
an umbrella, muttering
*I object. Maybe something bad
happened while you slept*,
they say. You get stranded,
an overpass like a bridge.

Please carry that sign in your arms.
A cloud around this wall I walk
like a road. A sign dissents
in English. I don't know how
to own my time. It's June
and it's July. How long do you look
for a fingernail clipping on the floor?
That wall is like a wall.

Have you and baby bonded,
they ask. That cave was like
a megaphone. I want a cigarette.
I want to be with you and

I want to be alone.
Detention centers.
All I want these arms to do.

WITH LOVE AND FLIGHT AND RAGE AND LOVE,

Some dispute the claim that it has no tense, only aspect.

Evening sour cherries
So much speech time
Billowing

Waiting does not want
To condense

"Is" cannot take a temporal aspect.

I worry your
Flight lines

To curio
The cats the coloring book

The three layers are speech time, reference time, and situation time.

Whether to conflate

An annual act
And situation time

Here is the world however
We destroy it

> *Unbounded events are located in the present.*

I keep confusing words
Husband and *bathroom*

Cast of a magpie
On the ground

Yellow flowers flush downward
With water

> *Bounded events are located in the past.*

I try to write at dusk
It's too heavy

Across a world
Wake so I can talk to you

The pine needles long on
The porch

The maddening
Embassy

> *No, bounded events are located either in the past or in the future.*

What world you will enter and I
Keep saying *sorry*

The blue tagine
On the stove

I am not quite multiple but

The block party's bounce pit
Out the front window

I hold you on
The orange couch

I write against birthdays

You bring back willow
Plums

> *"The plane takes off" has no natural endpoint.*

Sometimes I imagine you as bright
Purple fish

This shadow of zero

Alien addressee

Hot ambivalence at the binary
Running my insides

>*"Now I have a pet fish"* has no
>natural endpoint.

Fireworks while
We slept or from above

The first night instant noodles
Blown fuses

Golden tomatoes in the blue
Glass bowl

Children hoverboard

The magpie low

>*Any point can be the point.*

When the hours compress
I see day's shape

Where I stacked
The research books

Situation time's significance is [...].

Giddy how one place
Reminds us of others

Riled about
When we are now

Trying to accept it

I've had many careless raptures

I stand in the cool clean air
To mourn it

WITH LOVE AND FEAR AND RAGE AND LOVE,

We glare at an edge of epistolarity,
the grain of the date over distance.

It's not tempo it's not a gathering cry.
Fuck this new graffiti.

Promise gives me red sugar
but I'm lost in particulates,

air heavy under counting
and the weight of a week.

We love the old graffiti for its increase.
How it replies to itself.

The news says that they are
improvising assuming power.

Across the date, she is reading
about the sound of lynching.

It's not tempo this new graffiti.
It's carving absence it's scoring symbols.

By *new* I mean *current*
and by *current* I mean *hate*.

Whistling at night signals ghost
strikes. I keep trying to negate

into presence strike out strike
thorough strike with strike.

WITH LOVE AND TERROR AND RAGE AND LOVE,

I had a baby. Before, I wasn't sure
how to react when people said *You'll be*

a good mother. Like when my mother says
You potty trained so early because you were

so agreeable. It's true that having a baby
has made me more generous with

my social media likes and maybe more
ambidextrous in general. Also

that the everyday becomes akin
to camping, creaturely sounds hauling up

from sleep, fire feeding on my birthplace,
fire and flood and plastic and make do.

What world have I brought you to, that
you will have to spend your life in salvage.

*

In the hospital I keep thinking that
Plath line. After, I can't seem to say

I gave birth straight. I know
that this is bad thinking. Before, I'd had

a dream in which a friend demoed
a c-section with pumpkin and cleaver.

Then placenta secreted a cleft;
we packed and coiled ourselves as sunlight

slunk around the edges of the high-
rises. It was clear and crisp and blue.

I will myself wide but miss the deadline
and induction fails. *How could you*

know, the doctor says. From gurney, ceiling
tiles blink just like in the movies.

*

The placenta is heart-shaped, the midwife says.
In the hospital I'm naked for days,

abstract filmstrips playing at various speeds.
It's shaped like a heart. First I think the blood

is urine, catheter come loose perhaps
with other organs, a vague rupturing.

You test your dolphin language, your hilarious
vibrato. *Should I be losing this much blood*

I keep asking, groping toward time. You have
to contract to stop bleeding. The milk

comes on too strong so overnight they pummel
my tits and take away my soup. We rub

your ears to keep you feeding. Your tree frog phase.
I try to remember that you came to safety.

*

We wear each other like willows. Weeks
pass before I realize that while nursing

I can read sci-fi about the end of the world.
I become collector and arranger of

cushions, terrified of doorframes and
table edges. I can't remember the term

for *end of the world*. I try to look it up
but the VPN is down. I will admit:

you are an adorable asp on the tit.
The pink carnations drop their heavy heads,

the Italian teacher shuffles upstairs.
I'll call him Little Lucky, the midwife said.

Right: *apocalyptic*. What's the purpose
of this ever-diminishing recall?

*

The books all say that baby shit doesn't
smell that bad, but after a while

it smells like baby shit. A friend asks
what the indoor AQI is. *That's not*

that bad, he says. I am shocked the first
time I spew milk over the sheets. What

a grab bag, this existence. *It's like LA
on a really smoggy day.* I'm making

a selfish heap of nestled twilights.
We wait to hear whether a friend's father

has cancer. What world, endless shitty
news, turning toward your curtailed wail

in the dark. Afraid even to wonder
what kinds of persons you will be.

*

You startle like a supernatural being.
How breathing makes you dip. How sometimes

you vacate yourself. Your chest moving
forceful, something trying to get out.

The day before birth, your ribs on-screen
were like striated corset, interior

of the whale, cavernous cathedral,
motes in strips of light. How breathing

makes you bob, pulled by some private current
or otherworldly tide. I heard your heart

racing ahead, twisting, I first thought like
a horse but no, like a locomotive,

you are coming closer still and still
receding, a dusty distance dance.

WITH LOVE AND CAREER AND RAGE AND LOVE,

Distant verb, breakneck
verge. You learn pointing

and *in* and hiding.
At the window, a rare snow

sifts onto blue plastic
roofs through the

morning. I forget to
do Kegels, get some

grid. You eat a lucky
New Year's soup

after we pay to enter on
an incense day. Dear

country, dear emergency.
Your spine on-screen

so long. I think about how
when the gunshots began

most of the children ran
to the window.

Dear country, dear
emergency. You adore

ice and look good
in blue. Did I ever

know you? You try to buy
yellow chrysanthemums

and panicky language
ensues; they are funereal

and the powdered spheres
should be boiled first.

I have only
just started to

know again the meandering
pleasure of research,

of writing in the evening,
how you, dear

child, career (verb),
pleading without

language in the other
room. My (noun), long

clasped like a pearl in
the brain, bleats

and disintegrates.
Dear dear.

WITH LOVE AND CHROMA AND RAGE AND LOVE,

I pull the muted cream light over the cream
        bed and the cream curtain
and the cream book. The day diffuses.

I consider some advice to consider my grey
        hair when going on the market.
I pull the cream sky over my sternum. The word

for *sky* is the same as the word for *day*. I pull
        the cream light over the mint
cabinets. I pull it over the word *career* in my

teeth. What carries us. It's not quite canary.
        I get my period and an earache
and take up the blue pillows and pull the cream light

over my cuticles. I pull it over the cream tech buildings
        and a cream smokestack.
Diffused ambition is a burden and a relief.

I pull it over my cream porcelain cup and the cream cup's
        light yellow tea which is good
for the lungs. I pull it over a nuclear arsenal.

I remember my grandmother pulling up the cream
         blind to let in the cooler
cream light. Now the cream light gets more golden,

a little embarrassing, and I pull it over my throat and
         my pancreas. It gets richer
still and rosy and I pull it over an ache in my elbow.

I pull it over my follicles. I turn on a cream light
         and pick at some scabs
and turn it off. I pull it over a single sense

of direction. I am given a cream plush penguin
         and name it Adeline. I pull
the cream light over my toes and then over

my fuzzy mint slippers. I clutch Adeline whose cream
         stuffing begins to spill out
and I stitch it back in. I've been lying.

The book is more yellow than cream. The page
         is cream. The smokestack is more
beige than cream. Adeline is grey. I don't remember

her hand on the blind. She died several days hence
         two years ago. The building
has bands of cream but it cannot really be called cream.

I go into the room with the cream table and the different
            cream light. I pull it through
the cream glass made cream by condensation

that never leaves the panes. I pull it over my curved
            spine and my heavy forehead.
It would be easy to whittle it down. What's hard is

keeping things in. I pull it over a notebook from
            your student, whose name
on the cream cover is Antigone May.

I pull it over my gurgling viscera. I pull it over
            the houseplants that I care
about too much, which is perhaps why I have

been gifted Adeline. I pull it over my slightly pained
            armpits. I pull the cream
light between two high-rises where it is hiding,

the orange sun on the clothes porch. I pull it over the man
            lying still in the street
and how you said *don't look, we can't help.*

I pull it over the draft and my drafty brow.
            I pull it over the page
from which I keep walking away because the overflow

makes an echoing space in my chest. The cup is bone.
    Now the cream light is on
my temples. I pull it over our open eyes.

WITH LOVE AND BATHS AND RAGE AND LOVE,

        I go grasping
        with language &
            my plush
        body unravels.

    January, shitting
    blood in a Georgia
beach house,
        five months

        since last I wrote.
        A shutdown
            is not poetic.
        Did you leave

    to jot down
    a line, you ask.
No, I went
    to take my

blood pressure.
I write on
    WeChat,
hoping the bath

                is not too
                hot because I can't
Google a
                good source on water

                                temp. & pregnancy.
                                Fluid facts,
                                                willful walls.
                                I have applied to 48

                jobs. *We'll flip
                a coin,* you say, *to see
whose basement
                you'll live in.*

                                A freight train, a plane.
                                I should be
                                                applying
                                to a job right now.

                I hover over
                an article titled
*How to Rekindle
                a Friendship.*

PPD felt like
the personality
                dissociation
of strong salvia.

It's not repetition,
I say. We keep
looking for a way
      to want to stay.

           I imagine
           you as a tiny
                auger
           shell. What gets

    unraveled
    isn't form,
it's a form
    of supplication.

WITH LOVE AND DISTANCE AND RAGE AND LOVE,

    I stop believing in epistolarity

PEK to FOC

        Bodies at gates

FOC to TPE

    We cross the Tropic of Cancer
        Walk on marble sidewalks

            I think about crisis, travel, the unit of the day

    A clattering when the ocean crosses rocks

TPE to FOC

FOC to PEK

    Each of the tree species has a different posture and is well-worth appreciating

    But I am distanced now

        Statuary with sadness we

PEK to ORD

        Posture requires movement

                Dizzy at K2 instead of G6A
                Some basement gate

ORD to SDF

                Descent an ocean in the ear

        Imagining other airports

SDF to DFW

        Crying into breakfast tacos

                For weeks I've been trying to and running out
            of breath

                What I would give for a bathtub

DFW to PEK

                      The government watches us teach

      I'll clock the next person who says it's a good
      time to be gone

They want us statuary

          At least my organs keep moving, making

WITH LOVE AND FLIGHT AND RAGE AND LOVE,

The lilacs let out their nervy scent, you fall off a chair, I wash
my face with Speedy Perfect Whip
                                    It is morning, it is

my birthday, during which I have hacked
pregnancy I declare, splurging on small

satisfactions, drinking chai before biking the broken
pavement, a bit aggro, yelling *Too fast*, not ashamed

that I love the black hole photo, its feral eye, iris orange
and highlight too large like a bad touch-up
                                              In the afternoon

the new bathroom ceiling falls down and I drink
Earl Grey in class, feigning collapse over couplets,

thinking *levitate, leviathan* in the insistent light
at the square, concrete and grit, congregating

with the babies and the elderly
                                    I like to watch people
watch you and then we wrangle the evening

into place like pillows, thinking
self-soothing and *loose engagement*

while the moon, less yellow and winter-wide,
moves over the TusPark building
                              In the morning I sweep

for reports of the report and put on my protest socks
while you press up my skin, mining my hip and then

my rib, an irreducible state of matter
                                    I want a resilient age
and send thoughts to the placenta while

outside the office window the peonies
shout, so social, but by afternoon

I am ponderous and have hacked nothing
                                      You wake,
climb on the radiator pipes, point at the window,

your three cowlicks foretelling future
success, while we observe that blue seems to

have triumphed over yellow and orange in the bikeshare
battles, and you chart for us a way into evening where

I gather names and wonder whether to burden you
with kindness
              Perhaps I will miss even the grit,

like honey on hands, perhaps even sometimes
in the morning making tea, reading about the report,

biking past the pink-eared dog, the chickens, the woman
whacking her back with a ball
       They're your stories now,

he'd said, though he'd had different chickens in mind
than these behind the elementary school, watching

the white fuzz laze through the afternoon, slow sparks
outside my window, inverse to the third trimester floaters

everywhere drawing sight inward, *what universe within?*
   You order Blizzards and evening skirts toward

the island where you like to watch the dancers
and their brisk boundlessness, like red ribbons

on a flowering tree I try to show you while
walking home, thinking, *the scarlet conditions,*

wishing I'd made better use of our *yáng tái*, perhaps
even sometimes early in the morning, while I read

about the report and then the police come to the door
to scan our faces
     We talk about how the dancers sidestep

you and how almost three years later, many
restaurants are gone, and we all sleep

into early afternoon, until I wake wondering
what would it be like to be satisfied with my

cleverness?
          The time for the yellow flowers arrives
and goes and we point in the evening, *magpie, strawberry,*

mouth, knowing that next year we won't know spring
and looking to the time of naming to come

WITH LOVE AND NICE AND RAGE AND LOVE,

I sign about Ohio
before getting out
of bed. The ravens
get bold. They circle
in on keywords. When
it became clear
that we were low on
time they ushered
the male colleague
to the stage. You say
they talk to me to test
themselves. Please raise
your glass if you know
what resting nice face
does. The stage was
Shanghai. You say
continuity of self
is important to me.
So we get to the place
where I want to give
up on the poem.
Everything about Texas
is already Indiana. Here's
the thing about fetal
remains: it's tissue.

Place is a kind of
keyword. After he calls
Taiwan, you tell us
to register. This continuity
is curated. You say, *It's
when you let people lean
into you and then you
use their energy to
destroy them.* I try to
tell myself they can't
blast it back.
I use the form.
I set a time limit.
I excavate under nice.

WITH LOVE AND WILLFULNESS AND RAGE AND LOVE,

we buy a mattress   trying to solve it in the body

    Outside news time
    Beautification bulldozes along

I get my period   a bell against bone

    I say, *In English it's called*
    Postpartum depression

slow collisions of   grey

    Yes, you answer, *I've heard*
    The only thing that helps is your mother

city space   hollowed-out

    From the bus I see a man
    Stripping meat from a spine

used to trust some   senses

    You go face-first into tile
    I haul you up onto the bed

slow seconds   smear

Small mouth seeping red
Exquisite tedium

the height of lotus season

    I won't read this article about the orca
    And her dead baby

like addiction but less interesting

    Stop it, you say, *my situation*
    Is much worse than yours

can't help with connections

    Smooth my face
    Into a surface of balloon

won't say *refused* to break

    From the car a coat
    Black fur in the road

slow collusions of grey

    Finally I can see my brain
    A half-awake need not to die

you want *to have a try*

I don't want to live forever but
I do want a new bed

WITH LOVE AND LOCHIA AND RAGE AND LOVE,

the after plays trickster
    in labor

I walk long
    empty halls

continuing at night
    when I can't

find an edge
    chaos

join me nice
    you seal

your eyes against
    the sun

and we lie and
    say

you are one
    month

I see that
    comparison

is a kind
> of remembering

when you are
> my age

10% of the species
> will be gone

from the hallway I keep
> saying

I'm not here
> we bounce

down your head
> when they

let me off my back
> the day after

the night after the day after
> the night

I woke saying
> *I need*

you to see this
> water

falling on the floor
    or 25%

of the species
    will be

first I am scared
    to push

and then not
    you

smell unlike me
    your

forceps bruise
    lingers

I like the
    counting

am I still in those
    hallways

hundreds of
    thousands

march on an island
    as long

as there is progress
    he says

your exit an actual
    welcome

or 50% of the
    species

I take a selfie
    holding

you and pen to
    hold

myself more
    willing

wide spaces while
    our collective

engine whirs
    seven hours

behind you like the
    picture

you steady me when
    I am

embarrassed about the
    epidural

it's hard to hold
    these positions

there's a birth
    scene

on the wall that makes
    me sad

then not and
    safe

gloves beside
    the bed

I watch your
    eyelashes

come in
    fifteen

hours behind you
    like

the picture
    what ruins

shall we wander and
    will

the house hold us
    I worry

by temperament and
    training so

sometimes shrugging
    feels right

then the watermelons
    rolled

out of the car you say
    you try

on the playground
    to do what

the big ones do
    blurting

door and *dà*
    you bleat

your due date comes
    and goes

and does not cause
    grief

WITH LOVE AND LOVE AND RAGE AND LOVE,

A child got injured and a child got
sick. Children in caesurae. There

was waiting and then there was
moving. I sat in a hospital room

and seethed, sat on a white bed
while you slept in a plastic bin or

you slept on concrete. I read murder
mysteries because I couldn't bring

myself to fling stories into the
future. You hadn't been sleeping

on concrete but you had pneumonia,
or you didn't. On the facemask box

I expected *air* but instead the first
suggestion was *infant care*. I was

afraid for breath. I was afraid to
bring my face to your face.

WITH LOVE AND HORSES AND RAGE AND LOVE,

I should warn you I'm driving while emotional
Lacking armament for when

                                          Frantic for the photograph her hair
She was there where I unfurled
Wanting to wear any scrap a girl
                          A picture of a picture none of
                          them are
There the city river partly

Why aren't there more words for what's forgetting

I am casting for the question
Postpartum quarrying or
                    Ice fishing on the melt

Want you to tell me about then

We were always draped against
                            Windows I would gladly tell
                            you who
That girl was twenty-four
Bartering oblivion

This one's not easy she would've liked
Standing next to the nurse who asks *where's*

Anyone who would remember is far

                                          From the twentieth floor
                                              paper balloons

Smudges of light like in the play
Florescent paint was fireflies

That girl was twenty a forlorn
                                  Seeking aperture

I was not a brilliant student

Each eye contains a mirror
A pair she would've
                        Wanted to bring myself proximate to myself
The mirrors reflect blue light
                              I wish I had told her
The white of the eyes so white

WITH LOVE AND PATHS AND RAGE AND LOVE,

and all these months awake the hours the sky
begins to lift, become the inside of a shell,
our jagged memory and raveling
situated by sleep and its
absence

we let
first one and then
another place, goodnight Tianjin
goodnight Louisiana, your slick skin silk
small stay against a broadening uncertainty

goodnight Austin, your deeper blues and lighter
tans englassed in clear corneas, goodnight
Pingyao, red lanterns and a torn
duvet, a time
the threads

weft and fray, a
time where I become
a woman in her prime worrying
the minutes missed, vague about the scale,
attempting to frame yellow flashes everywhere

we go—desperate sociality or how much money
would we need to live here, grip checking
the circumference of my wrists,
I try to take a
picture

and a possible
friend departs, a dream
updated for our new design
wondering whether it is all trajectory
toward remodeling a kitchen and wanting that

antidote, the word she used, did I imagine it?—
or pregnancy, exhausted and opulent, but
now my pleasure relocates
and I am fucking
furious

flailing
for an antidote
indeed, the fibrous air
settles into days, polyester air,
getting close to all the shit, *la*, a note to follow

sew, the sun orange as on the morning of your
birth I open the news, raveling
goodnight dear children
murdered in
America

stay
here gaping at
a ceiling fan in Singapore,
liners bounding an ocean, goodnight
Singapore, I turn toward astrology for where

else can the future go—to flowers, which
Beijing at least knows how to do
or the actual flowers know,
bowed and lining
away.

WITH LOVE AND REMEMBERING AND RAGE AND LOVE,

I fall asleep pitching   into all

The places I've loved
All the addressees

        The partial correspondence
After

        I had babies I began   to conjure
                Ghosts in ceiling corners

Was it elegy?
Down the grey path   some tomatoes

We move to a city-state and I stop
        In the street

Before we left
I thought *description* for   weeks

Down the grey path some   pomegranates
        Was it pregnancy?

I knew I would miss

                The ramshackle

Your face crumples as
You turn back   into sleep

Ramshackle from an obsolete form
               Of *ransack*

I insisted on packing the blue deer
And the grey towel

          I wish I'd had more   mind

Down the grey path squash flowers
               Begin to climb

Was it Beijing?
Packing and description provoke   order

We packed   and packed

          Ransack from *house* and *seek*
Was it postpartum?

Workers pounded the paving stones
               With rubber mallets

          There is the order of time   and then

There is the order of the poems
Don't leave me in the house, I said

Is ending

Defying   time?
        Shower curtains on *hútòng* doors

An old man sees you and flashes
        A thumbs up

In the sideways I'd take
        The grey path

        We arrive and
I place you in sun

You said *sadness will enter*   *the breastmilk*

Did we stop
at detention centers?

I haven't taken anything Instagram-worthy
    Let alone   a line

        Another shooting
Circular news

It is   mothering time
I fear

        Fragile and

      A pool
The hue abundance

Did we to stop
At environmental rollbacks?

Maybe you have unrealistic expectations
For how much

      We remember about   our lives, you say

Did we stop
           At rainforest burning?

     An eyelid canvas pulsing
Peach and gold

The myna is not   a magpie
But it comes into the kitchen

           Steals a clothespin

Did we stop
At your water glee

Headlines   syncopated
Waiting for evening to see   morning

         Our hands holding

Shards   of sun?

APPENDIX: DATES

With Love and Dread and Rage and Love,: January 2017
With Love and Love and Rage and Love [1],: November 2016
With Love and Burrowing and Rage and Love,: December 2017
With Love and Guilt and Rage and Love,: July 2018
With Love and Flight and Rage and Love [1],: March/June 2017
With Love and Fear and Rage and Love,: November 2016
With Love and Terror and Rage and Love,: September–November 2017
With Love and Career and Rage and Love,: February–March 2019
With Love and Chroma and Rage and Love,: December 2016
With Love and Baths and Rage and Love,: January 2019
With Love and Distance and Rage and Love,: February–March 2017
With Love and Flight and Rage and Love [2],: March–May 2019
With Love and Nice and Rage and Love,: December 2016
With Love and Willfulness and Rage and Love,: August 2018
With Love and Lochia and Rage and Love,: June 2019
With Love and Love and Rage and Love [2],: August 2019
With Love and Horses and Rage and Love,: March 2018
With Love and Paths and Rage and Love,: May 2018
With Love and Remembering and Rage and Love,: August–September 2019

APPENDIX: ADDRESSEES

This writing was buoyed by what I wanted to tell you, Tristan Bates, Lauren Berlant, Phil Cordelli, Amanda Davis, April Faith-Slaker, Margaret Fink, MC Hyland, Cynthia Lin, Ricardo Maldonado, Kate McIntyre, Loretta Johnson, Cecily Parks, Sergio Preston, Lindsay Reckson, Joy Sun, Kurashige Taku, Kristen Tapson, Megan Tusler, Chalcey Wilding, Johanna Winant, Nicholas Wong, Erica Wright. And especially Richard, Gwendolyn, and Cassidy. Your motions mark the perimeters of home.

NOTES

Occasional lines in these poems come from addressee correspondence and news articles. Some italicized portions of "With Love and Flight," are from a lecture by Professor Sun Chaofen at Tsinghua University on April 28, 2017, in translation. "I've had many careless raptures" is from a December 18, 1970 letter by Larry Eigner to David and Maria Gitlin (University of Connecticut archives).

ACKNOWLEDGMENTS

I am grateful to the editors of the following publications, in which versions of these poems (including some not in this book) first appeared: *Burning House Press, Guernica, Posit, Sink Review, Spittoon* (Beijing), and *The Tiny*. A postscript to this collection can be found in *La Vague* 13, with a video poem version of that postscript on the Distāntia Remote Reading Archive.

STEPHANIE ANDERSON (she/they) is the author of three books of poetry, most recently *If You Love Error So Love Zero* (Trembling Pillow Press), as well as several chapbooks. She is also the editor of *Women in Small Press Publishing* (forthcoming Fall 2024, University of New Mexico Press), and co-editor of *All This Thinking: The Correspondence of Bernadette Mayer & Clark Coolidge* (University of New Mexico Press). An Assistant Professor of Literature & Creative Writing at Duke Kunshan University, she lives in Suzhou, China.

❉

COLOPHON

Text is set in a digital version of Jenson, designed by Robert Slimbach in 1996, and based on the work of punchcutter, printer, and publisher Nicolas Jenson. The titles here are in Futura, the best font for titles.

❊

NEW MICHIGAN PRESS, based in Tucson, Arizona, prints poetry and prose chapbooks, especially work that transcends traditional genre. Together with DIAGRAM, NMP sponsors a yearly chapbook competition.

DIAGRAM, a journal of text, art, and schematic, is published bimonthly at THEDIAGRAM.COM. Periodic print anthologies are available from the New Michigan Press at NEWMICHIGANPRESS.COM.

www.ingramcontent.com/pod-product-compliance
Lightning Source LLC
Chambersburg PA
CBHW022123040426
42450CB00006B/825